Foundations and policy involvement

Available in alternative formats

This publication can be provided in alternative formats, such as large print, Braille, audiotape and on disk. Please contact: Communications Department, Joseph Rowntree Foundation, The Homestead, 40 Water End, York YO30 6WP. Tel: 01904 615905. Email: info@jrf.org.uk

Foundations and policy involvement

Creating options

Diana Leat

**JOSEPH ROWNTREE
FOUNDATION**

The **Joseph Rowntree Foundation** has supported this project as part of its programme of research and innovative development projects, which it hopes will be of value to policy makers, practitioners and service users. The facts presented and views expressed in this report are, however, those of the author and not necessarily those of the Foundation.

Joseph Rowntree Foundation
The Homestead
40 Water End
York YO30 6WP
Website: www.jrf.org.uk

ISBN 1 85935 431 9   (paperback)
ISBN 1 85935 432 7   (pdf: available at www.jrf.org.uk)

A CIP catalogue record for this report is available from the British Library.

Cover design by Adkins Design

Prepared and printed by:
York Publishing Services Ltd
64 Hallfield Road
Layerthorpe
York
YO31 7ZQ
Tel: 01904 430033   Fax: 01904 430868 Website: www.yps-publishing.co.uk

Further copies of this report, or any other JRF publication, can be obtained either from the JRF website (www.jrf.org.uk/bookshop/) or from our distributor, York Publishing Services Ltd, at the above address.

CONTENTS

Democracy itself cannot bring about change, we first have
to provide the options.

> (*Trusting in Change: A Story of Reform*, Joseph
> Rowntree Reform Trust, 2004, p.1)

1 INTRODUCTION

Background

This paper focuses on foundations that seek to promote creative, constructive conversation and debate, with a view to influencing policy and practice in a variety of organisations and institutions at a variety of levels, achieving a sustainable impact beyond their immediate grantees.

The paper builds on previous case studies of foundations in the UK, US and Australia that have adopted this type of creative, policy-oriented approach (Anheier and Leat, 2006). These case studies are supplemented by further literature review and data from the Rowntree and other UK foundations with a view to providing a practical guide to creative, policy-oriented work.

Terminology

'Policy-oriented work' or 'engagement with policy' are deliberately loose phrases used here to refer to funding or undertaking work that is, or comes to be seen as, related to policy decisions in various organisations and institutions, including Government. 'Engagement with policy' occurs at a variety of levels from local to international and global. It takes various forms, from changing the way in which an issue is popularly viewed, to promoting democratic debate around issues, to more directly advocating for change; it may range from incorporating a particular practice into organisational or institutional policy through to more widespread policy change embedded in law.

In this paper, the term 'social justice philanthropy' is deliberately avoided for two main reasons. The first reason is that no foundation has as part of its mission statement the pursuit of social injustice, and most would probably claim to be 'righting wrongs' or in some sense redistributing resources from richer to poorer. Nevertheless, some foundation staff and trustees may attach overly radical connotations to the term.

If social justice philanthropy is defined as 'the practice of making contributions to nonprofit organisations that work for structural change and increase the opportunity of those who are less well off politically, economically and socially' (NCRP, 2003, p. 6), then the crucial difference seems to be an emphasis on structural change. If structural change is the issue, then, whatever the terminology and vision of what social justice looks like, the necessity to engage with public policy is common.

The second reason for focusing on policy engagement, rather than 'social justice philanthropy', is that the latter (as conventionally understood) excludes important lessons to be learned from foundations that have been effective in influencing policy and achieving structural change – most notably the US conservative foundations. (These foundations would be unlikely to describe themselves as committed to social injustice – rather they subscribe to a different analysis of what a just society would look like.)

Aims of the paper

Although there is nothing new about policy-oriented work by foundations, relatively few UK foundations aim explicitly to have an impact on policy and practice beyond their immediate grantees. However, there is growing interest in social-change, policy-oriented approaches in the US, the UK and wider Europe (see, for example, Burkeman and Harker, 2005; de Borms, 2005; Knight, 2005; Leat, forthcoming; Rosenman, 2005). This paper aims to show that policy involvement:

- is an important way of 'scaling up' and achieving sustainable impact

- is not political in the conventional sense, because policy making is not the sole province of politicians

- takes various forms and occurs at different levels and stages, with plenty of space for even risk-averse foundations to make a contribution

- is not radically different from what many foundations already do – what is needed is seeing work in a different light and following through

- involves resources other than money – resources that most foundations have or could develop

- requires strategies and skills that most foundations could easily adopt, as outlined and illustrated in this paper.

Structure of the paper

Chapter 2 outlines the roles of foundations and the arguments for and against getting involved in policy work. Chapter 3 discusses the policy process. Chapter 4 outlines what we know about the practices of foundations engaged in policy work. Chapter 5 explores the work of some UK foundations engaged in policy work, focusing in particular on the Rowntree trusts.

Chapter 6 discusses ways in which engagement in policy work differs from 'mainstream' foundation approaches and practices. The Appendix provides examples of the achievements of some policy-oriented foundations. A companion paper (in preparation), poses a series of practical questions and issues for foundations considering policy work.

2 ADAPTING TO A CHANGING WORLD: ARGUMENTS FOR AND AGAINST INVOLVEMENT IN POLICY ISSUES

Foundations in the UK have typically seen their roles in terms of service provision – providing immediate help to the needy/ disadvantaged. A smaller number have adopted a 'scientific approach', searching for the causes of problems (in the hope that understanding the causes would lead to adoption of appropriate solutions). In the US, there has been a strong tradition, among some of the larger foundations, of attempting to influence and inform public policy. However, during the last third of the twentieth century, a series of inquiries and 'reforms' encouraged foundations to focus on funding services. In the UK, while a larger number of foundations might claim to be concerned with social change, only a small number have adopted an explicit role in engaging with policy.

A recent study (Anheier and Daly, forthcoming) of roles and visions of foundations in Europe found that foundations in the UK were, for a variety of reasons, looking at ways in which they might adopt new roles and increase their effectiveness. Social and policy change was seen as one potential role but some staff were concerned about potential trustee resistance and about the foundations' resources and skills for the role (Leat, forthcoming).

Traditionally, there have been a number of arguments put forward against foundation involvement in public policy. These include matters of principle and practicality.

Arguments against policy engagement

- There is a clear dividing line between private 'charity' – providing services to the needy – and public policy; public policy is the preserve of Government, private charity is the preserve of foundations.

- Foundations do not have the moral/political right to trespass into the public policy arena.

- Foundations should stay out of public policy because involvement is prohibited by charity law.

- Foundations should stay out of public policy involvement because it diverts resources away from providing immediate help.

- Public policy involvement runs the risk of raising the profile of foundations, attracting conflict, criticism and greater regulation.

- Public policy work is too difficult/too costly/requires long-term commitment/cannot be assessed and involves high overhead costs.

- Public policy formation is too complex for foundations to grapple with.

The supposed difficulty of policy involvement is nicely captured by Michael Bailin, a US foundation president:

> … we were trying to reform huge, complex, entrenched, multibillion dollar public systems … that were fortified by all the ramparts of bureaucracy and regulation, and

thickets of intergovernmental agreements and contracts, and moats of public dollars. We were fighting battles that had tested the power and wealth of serial US congresses and presidencies. It was a battle of Homeric proportions fought with Lilliputian resources.

(Bailin, 2003)

But it seems that this is not an argument against policy involvement but rather one about timing. Bailin goes on to explain that, instead of trying to 'redesign the government sector', the foundation decided to focus on helping the best people in the sector to do what they want:

If it's good then it will require public dollars to have wider impact but that's a question for the future.

(Bailin, 2003)

Changing roles in a new environment?

The last sentence quoted above from Bailin expresses a fundamental truth about foundations' capacity for social impact and one that, at some level, foundations have always understood. In the last half of the twentieth century, foundations generally worked on the more or less explicit assumption that their very limited projects and programmes would be taken up by (local) government. Government, having been shown the need and the way, would replicate and fund foundation-generated projects. In other words, foundations would influence policy by the back door of quiet example.

Today that strategy is rarely available. Government has cast itself in the role of demonstrator and innovator; the role of non-

7

profits is to implement government priorities. Foundations may 'demonstrate' all they like but demonstration alone is no longer enough to ensure wider change and impact. This change in the environment in which foundations work is one of a number of arguments in favour of foundations' engagement with public policy.

More recently, the fashion for business metaphors and, closely related, capacity building have diverted attention away from foundations' roles in increasing social impact and achieving sustainable change via public policy work. Whereas businesses typically focus expansion efforts on organisational growth, foundations have other ways of achieving greater impact that involve letting go or spreading ideas rather than holding onto them. Businesses make money by retaining ownership of ideas and practices; foundations achieve impact by broadcasting ideas and encouraging others to take them up (see, for example, Kramer, 2005).

Arguments for policy engagement

- Arguments against foundations' engagement with policy are based on a misunderstanding of the processes of policy making and implementation. Foundations may contribute to policy formation and implementation in different ways, from problem definition to evaluation.

- There is no clear dividing line between private and public concerns in society today. Providing services to the needy and public policy are both processes of establishing social goals and distributing society's resources. Government is not something apart from 'us'; it is an instrument for shared public purposes and philanthropy has a role in increasing informed civic engagement and public participation rather than supporting the notion that individuals are powerless in the face of 'them', the Government (see, for example, Rosenman, 1998, pp. 28–44).

• Foundations have the same moral/political right to comment on and contribute to public policy as any other citizen/group in a democracy. Furthermore, foundation contributions to public policy processes may both enhance democracy by stimulating debate and contribute to the problem-solving capacity of society. Arguably, foundations have a moral responsibility to 'pay' for their lack of democratic accountability by enhancing democracy.

• It is a myth that contributing to public policy is prohibited by charity law – there is ample space within the law for foundations to contribute to public policy.

• Public policy involvement does not necessarily divert resources away from providing immediate help and, by investing in policy debate, foundations can increase the impact of their investment in direct services.

• More importantly, involvement in public policy work is a way in which foundations, given their relatively small financial resources (individually and collectively), can create sustainable change with an impact beyond their immediate grantees. Without wider social change, the work of foundations is restricted to short-term benefit for a lucky few grant recipients. All of the major US foundations founded in the early decades of the twentieth century – Russell Sage (1907), Carnegie (1911), Rockefeller (1913), Rosenwald (1917), Commonwealth (1918) – understood that they had to engage Government if they were to make a sustainable difference with impact beyond their immediate grantees.

- Researching/knowing the causes of something does not necessarily lead to change. Change requires both feasible, constructive solutions and political will that have to be built.

- Public policy involvement may indeed raise the profile of foundations and may attract criticism but these are mixed blessings and may, in any case, be the necessary concomitants of achieving their missions of sustainable change:

  The issue is not that foundations are policy-shy. They are controversy-shy and policy/advocacy is associated with controversy [but] investing in policy is essential to having an impact.

  (Thomas Layton quoted in Aron, 2002, p. 81)

- Public policy work may be difficult, uncertain and slow but, if it achieves wider, more sustainable change, then it may be no more uncertain, slow and costly than year after year of grantmaking to achieve short-term assistance that is constantly in need of renewal (see, for example, Aron, 2002, pp. 79–81).

- Without wider social change, philanthropy runs the risk of sustaining the problems it seeks to solve; social-change philanthropy seeks to reduce the demand for charity.

- Foundations have a moral responsibility to take a stand on public policy issues. If they do not, they 'risk coming under fire or, worse, becoming irrelevant' (de Borms, 2005, p. 76).

• Public policy work is complex but, as various foundations demonstrate, there are skills and techniques to be learned and it is not beyond the capacities of even relatively small foundations. (On foundations and public policy making generally see Ferris and Mintrom, 2002.)

Today it seems that engagement with public policy is coming back onto the agenda of foundations in both the UK and the US. In both countries, we seem to be emerging from a phase in which foundations acted as though they could somehow ignore Government (while, at the same time, implicitly relying on Government to provide ongoing maintenance for projects fathered by foundations). In the US, a country traditionally wary of 'strong' government, the following remark is significant:

> Foundations must finance long range efforts that enable nonprofit groups to understand that a strong government responsive and responsible to its people is essential to a strong civil society.
>
> (Rosenman, 2005)

Only Government, it is suggested, has the power to reduce the need for charity by appropriate exercise of its powers to regulate the way both public and private institutions operate (see also Heifetz *et al.*, 2004; Carson, 2005).

Before looking at the roles and strategies of foundations in engaging with policy, it is necessary first to outline the policy process.

3 THE POLICY PROCESS AND SPACE FOR FOUNDATIONS

Understanding the policy process not only provides the background for practice but also affects how foundations see their roles and limitations. If policy making is seen as something done solely by politicians, foundation influence may be somewhat constrained. If policy making is seen as something that involves a variety of institutions, actors and phases, then the legal and practical space for foundations to operate, and their points of access, are much greater.

Rational and political theories of policy making

Most people probably see policy making as a rational process based on a series of steps, from problem formulation and evaluation of alternatives through to policy implementation. This rational model sees the policy system as having clear boundaries; people identified as policy makers make policy (Gordon *et al.*, 1997).

One alternative model sees policy making as a process in which interests and perceptions of different actors enter at all stages. In this model it is more difficult to identify 'policy makers' and the boundaries of policy making. Policy making involves negotiations within the organisation and with a variety of others whose co-operation may be necessary for successful policy implementation (Gordon et al., 1997). Paradoxically, this political model may create more 'space' for foundations to be part of the policy-making process.

Problems, politics and policies

Kingdon (1984) takes understanding of the policy process a step further. He sees the policy process as involving three largely independent streams: problems, politics and policies.

- The problem stream concerns how and why states of affairs come to be considered problematic and involves factors such as the availability of systemic indicators, focusing on events including crises and disasters, and feedback from the operations of current programmes.

- The policy stream is analogous to biological natural selection: ideas float between communities of specialists and those proposals that meet certain criteria, including technical feasibility and budgetary workability, survive.

- The politics stream is affected by swings in the national mood, turnover of elected officials and interest from pressure groups.

- For Kingdon, the all-important coupling of these streams:

  ... is most likely when policy windows – opportunities for pushing pet proposals or conceptions of problems – are open ... windows are opened either by the appearance of compelling problems or by happenings in the political stream [while] ... alternatives are generated by the policy stream. Policy entrepreneurs, people who are willing to invest their resources in pushing their pet

> proposals ... are responsible not only for prompting important people to pay attention, but also for coupling solutions to problems and for coupling problems and solutions to politics.
>
> (Kingdon, 1984, p. 20)

Thus Kingdon's approach recognises that various participants:

> ... can all potentially be sources of, or indirectly affect, policy agenda items and alternative policy proposals, or 'solutions' to conditions which powerful actors sense are 'problems' and therefore merit a policy response.
>
> (Kendall and Anheier, 1999, p. 131)

Space for foundations

The discussion above highlights some key points.

- Policy formation is not the sole province of politicians.

- Policy does not just happen.

- There is a range of actors and stages and levels that provide points of access for foundations.

- Policy making and implementation is not a rational but a bargained, complex, messy process.

- For those reasons, policy formation and implementation is not entirely predictable.

- Policy does not flow from research/knowledge per se.

- Policy formation and implementation is a matter of competition between ideas.

- Ideas have to be marketed – they do not organically or 'naturally' communicate themselves.

- Political will for change has to be built.

If policy making is conceived of as a process – an ongoing conversation, involving a variety of stages and actors – then foundations have various points of access and tools to shape policy.

- They may attempt to influence the *problem stream* by carrying out and publicising research that highlights particular issues, reconceptualises them, presents them as at crisis level and/or provides feedback from operations of current programmes, and so on.

- They may attempt to influence the *policy stream* by promoting ideas and discussion, bringing together communities of specialists and others, and demonstrating the feasibility and workability of particular proposals.

- They may attempt to influence the *politics stream* by working on the national mood and/or by working directly or indirectly with, or building, other coalitions of interests and networks.

- Given the importance of the coupling of streams when policy windows are open, foundations need to be on the look out for 'open policy windows' (and ways of opening them) and then taking the opportunity to act as policy entrepreneurs.

- Foundations are unlikely to be able to influence policy alone. In attempting to influence the policy and politics streams in particular, foundations need to be aware of groupings of potential policy interests and partners, as potential obstacles to and allies in change.

- They need to work on and with other interests, building or participating in, for example, 'policy networks' and 'advocacy coalitions', made up of a wide range of actors, including Government from all levels, officials, interest organisations, research groups, journalists, and even other countries that share a belief system about a policy area and over time demonstrate some degree of co-ordinated activity (for further discussion see Leat, 2005b).

4 THE CHARACTERISTICS OF POLICY-ORIENTED FOUNDATIONS

In two publications (Anheier and Leat, 2002, 2006), foundations seeking to change the way in which social issues are viewed – and to stimulate creative, constructive conversation and debate via, among other methods, policy engagement – are described as 'creative foundations'. Creative foundations seek to change the way in which various target groups, including policy makers, think about and act on issues.

These foundations:

- see grantmaking as only the beginning of a usually long-term process and only one strategy in a complex toolbox

- start with a desired outcome that then indicates the initial strategy

- will do things themselves if necessary

- see policy making as the outcome of a complex contest of ideas in a competitive, crowded marketplace

- believe that the legitimacy and credibility of their contributions depends on an objective (non-party-partisan) stance

- emphasise the need to be outward looking, adaptive and flexible, and to work with others in a rapidly changing environment

- see knowledge, networks, influence and independent non-partisan voices as key resources

- work to build reputation and credibility, based on sound knowledge in a particular field

- draw out links between different programmes and combine knowledge derived from research and practice

- work to build rich networks of different types at various levels with a wide variety of other people and organisations in academia, the non-profit world, Government, the media and so on

- see social change as a matter of iteration, not cataclysm, requiring long-term commitment – believe that achieving social change requires work at various levels, with multiple strategies and tools

- spend time scanning the environment, keeping up with changes and spotting trends, newly opening policy windows and new issues

- juggle focus, for sound knowledge and rich networks, with flexibility, to take advantage of unforeseen opportunities, new points of access and leverage for change

- invest in communication to the right audiences by the most effective routes in the right format

- adopt a flexible and long-term approach to performance measurement and evaluation.

These characteristics of creative, policy-oriented foundations form a complex interrelated whole in which different elements inform and enhance each other.

Studies of US conservative foundations provide another source of data on what makes policy work effective. These foundations have been described as among the most successful foundations in history (see, for example, Smith, 2002; Roelofs, 2003 for the caveat that it is not difficult to be successful in encouraging conservative policy makers to adopt conservative ideas). They were not large in number, nor were they particularly wealthy. The effectiveness of conservative foundations has been related to:

- focus on building strong institutions by providing general, long-term, flexible operating support

- work at various policy levels with a mix of strategies and approaches

- investment in marketing of conservative policy ideas

- flexibility in the light of environmental change

- trust in grantees to do what is necessary, combined with a high level of interaction between foundations and grantees (Krehely *et al.*, 2004; and, somewhat differently, on characteristics of the Council on Foundations' Scrivner Award winners, see Brousseau, 2004).

5 THE ROWNTREE TRUSTS: POLICY WORK IN PRACTICE

This chapter relies heavily on the framework developed from a wider study of foundations in the UK, US and Australia (Anheier and Leat, 2006).

Approaches and achievements: overview

Joseph Rowntree Charitable Trust (JRCT)

JRCT describes its fundamental approach as responding to proposals from voluntary organisations, non-governmental organisations (NGOs) and think tanks, enabling them to achieve change in JRCT's priority areas. As a charitable organisation it is restricted to funding charitable purposes.

JRCT has played a significant role in Northern Ireland. Among other things, it funded the first integrated schools and was co-founder with the Nuffield Foundation of the Integrated Education Fund. In 1994 it founded Democratic Dialogue, Northern Ireland's first policy think tank. When the Good Friday Agreement was being negotiated in 1998, Community Dialogue promoted communication and debate on contentious political issues.

JRCT played a part in bringing into being: The Human Rights Act 1998, through its support for the key organisations in the Bill of Rights Consortium and, in particular, the Human Rights Incorporation Project; The Public Interest Disclosure Act 1998, through its support for Public Concern at Work; The Freedom of Information Act 2000, through its support for the Campaign for Freedom of Information. JRCT is currently funding individuals and organisations involved in the task force working with the Government to create a Commission for Equality and Human Rights. In addition, JRCT may be credited with getting a range of other ideas into the mainstream including the positive economic benefits of migration, community mediation, conflict transformation and peace building. Democratic Audit, publishing regular audits of the state of democracy in the UK, has been a flagship programme for ten years. In addition to these activities, JRCT also works in the fields of peace, racial justice, corporate responsibility and in South Africa.

JRCT attaches considerable significance to being a responsible shareholder and has been influential in creating and encouraging support for the Ethical Investment Research Service (EIRIS).

Joseph Rowntree Foundation (JRF)

Despite its frequent designation as a 'research foundation', JRF does not fund the pursuit of knowledge for its own sake but rather for its capacity to change policy or practice for the better. 'Search and change' is one of its key phrases. As a charitable organisation it is restricted to funding charitable purposes. JRF's traditional approach has been to work with partners (grantees) to produce research evidence for change; more recently, it has adopted a role in building on research via policy and practice development programmes on selected themes.

JRF has been influential in recent policy developments in its focus areas of poverty and place. A central ingredient of JRF philosophy – mixing incomes and tenures in housing – is now part of national policy. Similarly, JRF's interest in civil responsibility is now part of government policy on active citizenship and active communities. JRF was involved with the creation of the Social Exclusion Unit and with the National Strategy for Neighbourhood Renewal and wider work on area regeneration, informed by, among other work, its Action on Estates programme. A variety of reports have sought to influence policy on poverty; and, at the end of the 1990s, Government committed to abolish child poverty in a generation. The development of Tax Credits — redistributing resources to poorer working households – has been influenced by the work of JRF. Work on family policy over 25 years has had important impacts on policy in relation to work–life balance and divorce and separation. JRF was influential in the creation of SureStart and worked closely with the Government on early implementation.

Work on social care and disability has been influential in changing public attitudes and in creation of the policy of Direct Payments for those who want to arrange their own care provision. A ten-year research programme on local governance culminated in a summit at Leeds Castle in 1996 for a number of leading policy makers who considered the relationships between central and local government.

JRF's recent interests include drugs and alcohol, governance, immigration and inclusion, independent living, and parenting. In 2004, JRF announced a new Public Interest in Poverty Issues programme.

Joseph Rowntree Housing Trust (JRHT)

JRHT is the operational arm of JRF. It shares trustees, chief officers and administration with JRF. With income in 2004 of £11.6 million it is the largest of the four trusts, and manages 2,000 housing properties in New Earswick, the City of York and surrounding areas. JRHT is not just about housing – it aims to create inclusive, mixed-income, cohesive neighbourhoods. To this end it has experimented with new approaches to design, tenure, management and finance. JRHT seeks to demonstrate new approaches and to promote innovation by testing practical solutions. Through the JRF's publicity and dissemination mechanisms, it seeks to have an effect nationally on housing and neighbourhood policy.

JRHT can claim credit for a number of policy and practice innovations. It demonstrated the value of more accessible homes with its 'Lifetime Homes' standards, a number of which have been incorporated into the national standards for all new housing developments. It invented Flexible Tenure arrangements that allow home buyers to sell back equity shares if their needs change, and has been a leader in developing mixed-income communities with its Sales of Alternate Vacants on Estates (SAVE) scheme. It has been a pioneer in the field of continuing care, developing the UK's most comprehensive Continuing Care Retirement Community. It has also supplied a test bed for a new flexible skill mix for providing nursing and social care within a single care home: this work has been carried out in co-operation with the Commission for Social Care Inspection with a view to informing a review of the regulatory process.

In managing its own properties, JRHT has developed participatory models of governance and is experimenting with ways of reducing intergenerational conflict with projects that reward young people who help their community, and Communities that Care encouraging local people to support projects promoting young people's achievement in school and reducing problem behaviour.

Joseph Rowntree Reform Trust Ltd (JRRT)

JRRT is the 'odd one out' in that it is the only one of the four trusts without charitable status and thus free to engage with the policy process without any legal constraints. Its political and campaigning work is central to its role. JRRT describes itself as 'a Risk Taker, capital R, capital T' (personal communication). Most, if not all, of its work is about policy change, focusing in particular on 'the continuity of reform within the democratic system':

> JRRT aims to correct imbalances of power, strengthening the hand of individuals, groups and organisations who are striving for reform.
>
> (personal communication)

One of the directors describes JRRT as a 'bucaneer for democracy'. JRRT has funded almost every constitutional reform group in the UK, supporting groups, pursuing devolution, constitutional change and democratic reform, whilst playing a role at various points in history in creating/strengthening democracy in Africa, Northern Ireland and wider Europe. Among many other achievements, JRRT was an early funder of the National Council for Civil Liberties (now Liberty) and was one of the first funders of Solidarity.

JRRT is not committed to the policies of any one political party, and has supported individual politicians and groups promoting new ideas and policies from all the major parties in the UK. Direct party support has only been given when the directors have judged that particular political developments should be fostered, especially those central to a healthy democratic process such as constitutional and electoral reform. Grants 'aim to encourage a positive exchange of views and ideas amongst those involved in the political process, to redress the balance of financial inequality between the parties and to stimulate radical change'. Grants may be made to non-party pressure groups and other organisations that cannot seek charitable funding, but need assistance for particular purposes in the short term, and to 'effective individuals' identified by JRRT. One example of this strategy is JRRT's provision of research support for leading frontbenchers to improve the quality of parliamentary opposition. (The scheme was formally incorporated into the workings of the House of Commons in 1974; and many of the people supported went on to become leading policy figures.)

One example of the way in which JRRT has 'strengthened the hand' (a phrase from Joseph Rowntree's Memorandum) of others is The State of the Nation Polls examining public attitudes to a number of issues connected with the constitutional and democratic reform agenda, enabling grantees and others to detect shifts of opinion and use the results in support of their arguments. More recently, JRRT has been influential in Electoral Commission recommendations for reform of funding political parties, and has created (and funded with JRCT) the POWER inquiry into the future of British democracy.

Similarities and differences

Background: similarities, differences and diversity

The Rowntree trusts are some of the best-known policy-oriented funders in the UK. The trusts illustrate different styles and approaches to policy-oriented work while, at the same time, demonstrating that policy-oriented foundations share some common family resemblances relative to 'conventional' foundation approaches.

The trusts share a common father, a common guiding memorandum and a common set of fundamental values. JRRT and JRCT share a building and one common trustee. JRF and JRHT share both trustees and administration. Most obviously they differ in their focus (as outlined above). They differ in size, ranging from JRHT's £11.6 million income to JRRT's income of just over £1 million. Differences in size of income partly explain differences in how and what the trusts fund. The trusts also vary in the proportion of income allocated to grantmaking. The most obvious contrast here is between the JRHT, devoting all of its income to its own operations, and the other three trusts, which give a proportion of their income in grants to others. But there are also differences here between the three grantmaking trusts, with JRF spending a larger proportion of its income on in-house staffing and activities compared with JRRT and JRCT. Differences in proportions of income devoted to grantmaking reflect a more fundamental difference in approach and style. These differences are discussed further below but it is worth commenting here that, on a continuum from grantmaking to operating, JRHT would be clearly at the operating end, JRCT very close to the grantmaking end and JRRT and JRF at points in between. (However, it is important to note that categorising by spending is different from categorising by time spent.)

The trusts differ in styles of governance, reflected in part in the different titles of the chief manager in each trust. Trustees of the JRCT and JRRT play a more direct hands-on role than those of JRF, who appear to delegate greater responsibility to paid staff.

Although the trusts share some common Quaker values, they vary in their identification. For example, while JRCT sees itself very clearly as a Quaker trust, and all of its trustees are Quakers, JRF (with a constitutional link to the Society of Friends) does not do so in the same way. Again, this is in part a reflection of the different approaches and activities of the trusts, with JRF placing more emphasis on 'objective' research knowledge than the other three trusts (which also value, and spend, on knowledge but define it more broadly).

But there are dangers in focusing on the trusts' differences. One danger is that the common characteristics and strategies that make the 'family' different from the majority of UK foundations and contribute to their effectiveness as policy shapers are neglected.

There is another danger. Focusing on differences and/or on similarities underplays the complexity of the trusts' approaches and work and the diversity *within* each trust, and over time. So, for example, while JRF is primarily research oriented, it also does policy and practice development; while JRCT primarily responds to policy-oriented proposals from others, it also takes initiatives of its own and, in addition, sometimes funds research. The diversity within each trust, and the overlaps between them, are demonstrated most obviously when they fund the same organisation – albeit often for different aspects of work or in different ways (e.g. core versus project funding). Diversity of tools and strategies within a foundation is one important characteristic of policy-oriented foundations.

The discussion below highlights common themes in order to draw out characteristics of policy-oriented work, but also attempts to do justice to the important differences in emphasis and diversity between and within the trusts. One way of achieving this tricky task is to place the trusts on continua of emphasis on different roles and styles. The continua below attempt to highlight both the differences between the trusts and their difference from the 'generality' of UK trusts. There are two difficulties here. One is that the Rowntree trusts may disagree with their positioning on the continua – but if the continua stimulate debate and serve as a tool for clarifying similarities and differences that may be valuable in itself. The second difficulty is that the 'generality' of UK trusts is an overgeneralisation. A small number of trusts would need to be arranged carefully along each continuum interspersed with the Rowntree trusts, for example the Cadbury trusts; Nuffield Foundation; the Diana, Princess of Wales Memorial Fund; Esmee Fairbairn Foundation; Carnegie UK Trust, among others. Nevertheless, and with apologies to those other trusts, the continua may be useful as a heuristic device.

Family resemblance in roles

What makes the trusts different from the majority of UK foundations? One answer is that all four trusts use their independence to adopt the roles not of charitable givers but of:

- knowledge entrepreneurs/generators and organisers of new thinking

- risk absorbers

- social issue entrepreneurs

- brokers and convenors (Anheier and Leat, 2006; on the convenor role see de Borms, 2005).

These roles are strategies towards stimulating debate, demonstrating opportunities for change and building the necessary public and political will for change that will have a sustainable impact beyond immediate grantees. Emphasis on each role and the extent to which roles are played out directly by the trust, or primarily via grantees, varies between the trusts.

Knowledge entrepreneurs

Figure 1 Emphasis on knowledge generation

High _____ Low

      JRF   JRHT   JRCT   'Generality' of UK trusts

                      JRRT

The trusts vary in their emphasis on knowledge generation and the type of knowledge produced. For example, JRF works primarily with grantees who can deliver sound credible knowledge, whereas JRCT talks about working with grantees who have 'a money-shaped gap'. In the latter case, the organisation may have knowledge but lack the networks effectively to use that knowledge.

When JRRT created the Acton Society (an early think tank) to analyse the implications of the welfare state for liberty and the individual, the aim was to 'foster a more reflective capacity for comprehending issues on the public agenda' (JRCT *et al.*, 2004, p. 8), an aim that could be used to describe the other trusts' roles. More recently, JRRT funded a series of State of the Nation surveys to monitor public opinion on a range of democratic issues, helping both to put constitutional matters on the public agenda and to shape informed comment on such matters, and initiated the POWER inquiry, with JRCT, into the future of British democracy.

All four use their independence to 'think outside the box', to generate new ways of seeing old issues and to provide informed approaches to new issues.

One example of thinking outside the box is JRCT's centennial project Visionaries for the Future, providing £1.6 million to release six individuals to work for the promotion of peace and justice in society. As it did not want the funding to go to established 'experts', the Trust placed an open advertisement for proposals acknowledging that (as research demonstrates) innovation most often comes from outside the mainstream (see, for example, Coleman *et al.*, 1957; Kanter, 1983; Kanter *et al.*, 1992; Landry, 2000).

All of the trusts combine an emphasis on thorough knowledge and understanding, with space for opportunism, 'acts of faith' and 'leaps in the dark', maintaining flexibility for more new thinking.

Risk absorbers

Figure 2 Risk tolerance

High _____ Low

JRRT	JRCT	JRF	'Generality' of UK trusts
		JRHT	

All four trusts are willing, in varying degrees, to take risks and tolerate controversy.

Non-charitable JRRT describes itself as 'a Risk Taker, capital R, capital T' and has supported a range of radical political (and other) causes in the UK, Africa, Northern Ireland, and wider Europe. JRCT has a record of backing often controversial projects, many of which later move into the mainstream, for example Campaign for Freedom of Information, Integrated Schools in Northern Ireland, Public Concern at Work, The Glidewell Panel of enquiry into the implications of the 1995 Asylum and Immigration Bill, and work done by the Human Rights Incorporation Project in influencing the drafting of the Human Rights Act.

All four trusts are willing to absorb risk by taking the lead and doing things themselves where necessary (e.g. where there is no suitable grantee).

Although there is a variety of risks for grantmaking trusts other than political risks (Leat, 2005a), political risk is a key consideration for charitable trusts. This raises a wider issue about trusts' relationships to Government. The 'generality' of UK foundations do not see (or have not traditionally seen) their role as relating to Government, other than to stress their independence, while often, in effect, providing services that reduce the burden on Government. Policy-oriented trusts necessarily take a position on relationships with Government.

All four trusts relate to Government but differ in the style they adopt. JRRT's relationship with Government is one of open challenge. This is not simply because it is a non-charitable trust but also because its role is to ensure an informed and vibrant opposition as part of a functioning democracy. JRF and JRHT are concerned not so much with the infrastructure of democracy but more with influencing government policy on specific issues and they therefore tend to adopt the more amicable role of 'objective informer' and 'persuader'. JRCT's approach is more complex, working, as it does, through grantees who may adopt persuader or challenger roles.

Figure 3 Relationship to Government

Open challenge _____ Informer/persuader _____ Charitable helper

JRRT   JRCT   JRF*   JRHT   'Generality' of UK trusts

* Interestingly, JRF may be moving further to the left of the continuum with its Public Interests in Poverty Issues (PIPI) programme.

Social issue entrepreneurs

Figure 4 Social issue entrepreneur

High _____ Low

JRF   'Generality' of UK trusts

JRCT

JRHT

JRRT

Unlike some other foundations, the trusts have not stopped with the generation of knowledge but have combined that with emphasis on 'providing the options', putting issues on the social agenda via experimentation, active dissemination and use of networks and influence.

The trusts differ in emphasis on how they spread new ideas. Funding pressure groups has been one means of getting issues onto the agenda for both JRRT and JRCT.

> JRRT was one of the earliest funders of both the Child Poverty Action Group (CPAG) and Amnesty. In recent decades JRRT has devoted considerable attention to constitutional reform. In the 1970s and 1980s it supported centres for campaigning, research, thinking and policy on constitutional reform as well as the Scottish Constitutional Convention and Charter 88, the latter viewed as one of the most successful pressure groups of the 1990s. Similarly, JRCT has successfully supported the Campaign for Freedom of Information to campaign for the FoI Act, Public Concern at Work for legislation on whistleblowing, and the Centre for Corporate Accountability for legislation on work-related deaths.

JRF adopts a slightly different approach, working to (re)define problems and get them onto the wider social agenda by testing out new ideas (ensuring the details of successes and failures are available to all), a rigorous dissemination policy, contributions to policy debates on the basis of extensive research funded by JRF and support of inquiries. JHRT adopts similar strategies based on its own experience and experiments in developing new forms of housing.

Brokers and convenors

Figure 5 Use of brokering and convening

High _____ Low

| JRF | JRCT | 'Generality' of UK trusts |
| | JRRT | |

The three grantmaking trusts see brokering and convening as a key role. JRF sees brokering and convening as one of its major roles and often uses advisory groups, inquiries and commissions as a way of convening and brokering, bringing people in, getting perspectives and creating networks. JRRT states that: 'It seeks to foster creative intervention by anticipating and brokering change within the body politic' (www.jrrt.org.uk). This is a view that might also be ascribed to JRF and JRCT.

JRF has created or supported Inquiries and Commissions. The Duke of Edinburgh's Inquiry into Housing, the JRF Inquiry into Income and Wealth and the 2004 Commission on Good Governance in Public Services (with the Chartered Institute of Public Finance and Accountancy and the Office of Public

(Continued)

Management) are examples of this role in action. The JRF New Communities Network is bringing together those facing the challenges of easing housing shortages and mixed-income new communities. Similarly, JRF and JRHT are working with others to spread the idea of continuing care retirement communities.

One example of JRRT's convening/brokering role was in the 1970s when media ownership and control was a major issue. JRRT brought together a number of pressure groups under the umbrella of the Standing Conference on Broadcasting to defend the principles and practice of public service broadcasting (leading to the Annan Commission).

JRRT played a somewhat different convening role when it created 9 Poland Street as a home for a wide array of pressure groups spanning the social and political spectrum. It was described in the press as being the centre for '"the counter civil service" which it was for much of its twenty years incarnation' (JRCT et al., 2004, p. 11). Poland Street created networks, built institutions and promoted alternative thinking. Again, JRRT supported New Society and brokered its merger with the New Statesman in order to maintain one left of centre weekly journal for analysis and comment. More recently, it has been active in bringing people together to respond to the rise of the British National Party (BNP), creating (with JRCT) the POWER inquiry and in promoting state funding of political parties.

In its work on The Human Rights Act, JRCT adopted a hands-on role 'encouraging organisations to cooperate and carve out individual areas of expertise' (Davies, 2004, p. 281). JRCT notes that:

> We regularly fund people who would have difficulty talking to each other, and that may mean we can bring them together – even if we didn't fund them in order to do that.

Brokering and convening raise difficult issues about neutrality and taking positions. These are discussed further below.

Similarities and differences in strategies and tools

Each of the trusts uses a complex mix of strategies and tools with different degrees of emphasis. Again, this mix is somewhat different from that used by the 'generality' of UK trusts.

Clear values for focus and flexibility

Although the trusts vary in the extent to which their values and philosophy are publicly articulated; they all demonstrate vision, passion and long-term commitment derived in different ways from Joseph Rowntree and Quaker values. However, they differ in their focus on different aspects of those values.

JRRT is clearly focused on building and maintaining the institutions of democracy, JRCT on promoting peace and justice, and JRF and JRHT primarily on social inequality

(Continued)

35

> focusing on poverty and housing. There are also crossovers –
> for example, JRF's interest in good governance has obvious
> relationships with JRRT's emphasis on institutions of
> democracy and JRCT's focus on corporate responsibility and
> democratic participation in supporting, for example, Operation
> Black Vote.

Whatever the differences in articulation and focus, the trusts
have in common a strong value core providing the basis for focus
and long-term commitment to chosen issues (on the importance
of a strong value base see also Knight, 2005). All four trusts stay
with chosen issues long term. All accept that, in policy work,
'miracles take longer' and believe in 'the patience of ideas'. At
the same time, a strong value base allows flexibility without
incoherence.

> For example, in order to retain flexibility, JRRT (unlike JRF
> and JRCT) does not have themed programmes of work. But
> it argues:
>
> > The clear sense of liberal values and righting the balance
> > of power that underpin the work of the Trust ensure that
> > our grantmaking does not descend into incoherence.
>
> Similarly, JRCT emphasises the value of flexibility and
> 'discernment':
>
> > We want to be open to people and organisations with
> > passion who are thinking creatively. What we don't want
> > to do is place obstacles in their way. Informed
> > discernment is a good description of how we operate.

A theory of change

Although the trusts' theories of change differ, the important point is that they work with more or less explicit theories of change – even if part of the theory is that circumstances alter cases.

No magic bullets

All of the trusts subscribe to the view that there is no magic bullet, no one way of achieving change. Change strategies have to be adapted to circumstances and issues.

Change changes

Theories of change are also subject to debate and review in the light of changing social and political structures.

> For example, whereas in 1937 Rufus Jones wrote that he pinned his hopes on 'quiet processes and small circles in which vital and transforming events take place', JRCT now asks whether this is applicable in the light of the bureaucratic complexities of the European Union, the need for international agreements and legal frameworks that are increasingly obscure to laymen and politicians.
>
> (JRCT *et al.*, 2004)

Knowledge is not enough

One common thread in the trusts' theories of how change can be achieved is the acceptance that research to establish causes is not enough.

> … poverty itself has not been eradicated, though the root causes are known. What is lacking is the political will to deal with it.
>
> (JRCT *et al.*, 2004, p. 32)
>
> *(Continued)*

Similarly, the very fact that JRF has clearly designated Policy and Practice Development (PPD) programmes is significant in underlining the fact that research/knowledge is not enough to create policy and practice change. Facts do not speak for themselves (and are sometimes inconsistent) and, in addition, changing both policy and practice involves having practice wisdom.

In the past, JRF has probably placed more faith in the power of knowledge/'facts' than the other trusts. Today, it is questioning whether, in order to be more effective in achieving change, it should adopt a more assertive approach in which it is 'independent but not neutral', thus coming closer, in some ways, to the position of JRCT and JRRT.

Beyond rationality: incentives and disincentives

Proposing rational solutions does not necessarily achieve change.

For example, the aim in work on migration is not simply to produce a just and rational immigration policy. The challenge is far more complex. It is how to provide a just system that has some chance of being adopted and of surviving in the context of the prejudice that exists which is being fermented by the tabloid press, the political pressure this creates and the reflex that seems to impel politicians to respond by demonstrating toughness to the point of ruthlessness. Logic and rationality are not enough for this.

(S. Pittam, JRCT unpublished paper)

(Continued)

Similarly, JRF recognises that change that is not in the interests of those currently in charge is likely to be resisted. Ownership of the problem may not be enough if this conflicts with self-interest. There is then a need to remove disincentives and maximise incentives, using sticks of instruction or regulation, or carrots of financial and other incentives. Resources can be one powerful incentive to change; in that case change involves reaching those who regulate, instruct or pay. In this the centralised character of British Government can help in narrowing the targets for a change agenda.

One potentially persuasive characteristic of some JRF-funded research reports is the inclusion of *costed* proposals for change and/or the tangible financial costs of failing to change. Similarly, JRHT's demonstration of new ways of designing housing and care, and the costs of that, are an important tool in removing obstacles to change.

Working for and against

For JRRT, policy work has two faces: positive policy work to develop new ideas to improve matters, and negative work to prevent undesirable legislation coming into force or to modify it sufficiently to curb its effects. In some cases, JRRT's funding may work to bring an issue onto the policy agenda; in other cases, the aim may be to keep an issue from dropping off the agenda.

Change is a long-term process

All of the trusts accept that achieving change is most often a long-term process requiring more sustained commitment than is usual in many foundations. As a result of this, all have stayed with issues – and in many cases particular grantees – over decades.

For example, JRCT has been working on migration issues for over 30 years and JRF and JRHT have worked on housing since their inception. Underlying the practice of long-term funding for issues, and often grantees, is recognition, shared by all three trusts, that achieving social change is a long-term process.

Long-term commitment to an issue and ongoing research has important effects on the effectiveness of communication, creating an 'echo chamber' of messages far more effective than one message, however strong, could be.

For example, the JRF Inquiry into Income and Wealth backed by research in 16 universities was regarded as hugely influential on public opinion. Since then, JRF has published a report each year from the New Policy Institute to track progress (*Monitoring Poverty and Social Exclusion.*)

There are also differences in style. JRCT and JRRT have a record of providing core operating support for a range of organisations; JRCT also tends to provide longer-term support, giving some organisations sufficient by way of core costs and infrastructure funding to enable them to work on complex issues for long periods of time (15 years or longer), ready to take advantage of a window of opportunity to influence the policy debate. While JRF and JRRT stay with issues long term, they do not make a practice of staying with particular grantees long term (although both may return to previous grantees).

Flexibility and opportunism

Flexibility to adapt to a changing policy environment requires flexibility and opportunism within the foundation and grantee organisations. The importance of opportunism, or 'timeliness', is acknowledged by the trusts.

JRRT links opportunism to good value; it looks for 'those ideas whose time has come, or is about to come, and offers small amounts of money (as well as sometimes quite large amounts) at the moment when it judges that the most positive results can be achieved'. JRF talks about the PPD approach as about turning the 'vision into reality now that the political tide is flowing in favour of JR's approach' (JRCT *et al.*, 2004, p. 20). JRCT talks about bringing different strands of work together, 'especially when a window of opportunity arises to create change'. (Interestingly, Davies [2004, p. 283] attributes a large part of JRCT's success in relation to freedom of information and human rights to timing, but suggests that this may have been serendipitous rather than deliberate.)

(JRCT *et al.*, 2004)

Although 'timeliness' regarding government agendas is a consideration in funding decisions, the trusts share a belief in the importance of retaining the freedom to do something that is not topical. Balancing flexibility and opportunism with strategic direction and focus can be tricky; this is a dilemma the three grantmaking trusts grapple with.

Styles of support: flexibility and control, core and project funding

Adapting to a changing policy environment requires that foundations are fleet of foot. There are various ways of achieving this. One way is to rely on grantees, supporting individuals and/ or giving core operating support rather than project funding.

JRCT and JRRT, in particular, have made a practice of supporting individuals and organisations to work in ways they see fit, allowing considerable freedom to pursue developing issues in a changing policy environment. This has two key aspects: supporting individuals and providing core funding to organisations.

Examples of individual support include JRRT's provision of research support for leading frontbenchers, designed to improve the quality of parliamentary opposition. Similarly, JRCT has funded some individuals it sees as particularly effective as they move from post to post.

JRCT and JRRT frequently give core funding to organisations. JRRT states that it likes grantees to 'work in their own ways'. JRCT talks of 'having faith in key people and key organisations, often ones that work across a range of issues, and staying with them' and describes its relationship with grantees as that of 'critical friend' challenging groups to stay on target. JRCT may work with an organisation to redefine strategy or assess impact but attempts to do this through negotiation rather than enforcement: 'We are interested in power with rather than power over ... liberating groups to take risks and to follow their vision'.

Davies (2004) attributes a large measure of JRCT's success in influencing policy to its funding of grantees' research and administrative capacity and a 'principled investment in the talents of individuals and organisations' (Davies, 2004, p. 283; on the importance of 'vision, people and flexibility' see also Kilmurray, quoted in de Borms, 2005, p. 90).

Another way of being fleet of foot in a changing environment is to take responsibility for spotting issues and maintain flexibility via project funding.

JRF tends to take responsibility itself for spotting issues and responding to changing environments. JRF typically commissions pieces of research and enters into 'partnerships' with those it supports. Funding is most likely to be carefully specified and time-limited. In some cases JRF, and for example JRCT, may support the same organisation but, while JRCT funds core costs, JRF is much more likely to provide funding for a particular project.

These differences add up to different approaches to the way in which the grantmaking trusts relate to those they fund, and in how they fund.

Figure 6 Styles of support

(Trust-initiated, time-limited, specified project)   (Responsive, loosely specified core)

Commissioning _____ Grantmaking

*   JRF   JRCT

                                            JRRT

* The 'generality' of UK trusts does not fit easily here, tending to give responsive but time-limited project support.

Work at a variety of levels and different tools

All of the trusts have worked at local, county, regional and national levels, and JRRT and JRCT, in particular, have worked at European and international levels.

JRCT emphasises the value of working across boundaries of grantmaking strands, making links 'to capitalise on this cross-fertilisation and to work at a variety of levels – grassroots, regional, national and European – and in several different ways – advocacy, policy, lobbying and visionary' (JRCT *et al.*, 2004, p. 36).

In its work on migration, JRCT has combined work at local, national and European levels. It supported work on the impact of policy on local communities (e.g. publication of *Dispersed* in 2001 looking at the effects of the Government's dispersal policy on services available for West Yorkshire asylum seekers). At the national level, it supported the Runnymede Trust's work on the implication of asylum and immigration policy for British society. At the European level, JRCT supported work by the Migration Policy Group with the Immigration Law Practitioners' Association (ILPA) and the European Council on Refugees and Exiles, influencing the drafting of the first European directives on asylum, migration and integration.

Similarly, JRF and JRHT's work on housing and social care has been conducted at local and national level. For example, JRF may work with JRHT to take a local New Earswick project to national level. Lifetime Homes and flexible-tenure housing are both examples of the move from local to national level.

The trusts also use a variety of tools to achieve their goals, both within each trust and between the trusts.

While JRF has tended to focus on research, communication and convening as its key tool mix, JRCT mixes tools by funding 'organisations operating on both the outside and inside tracks

(Continued)

– groups proposing radical solutions as part of a long-term vision, and other groups working to influence short-term government policy. We fund think tanks and campaigning organisations working on the same issue'. (On mix of tools see also de Borms' [2005, pp. 63–8] description of the way in which grants, citizen mobilisation, research and policy advocacy were used to create a multiplier effect in the King Baudouin Foundation's Architectural Heritage Programme.)

Operating and grantmaking

Among foundations, and in the literature, grantmaking and operating tend to be seen as very distinct styles: foundations are one or the other. While JRHT is clearly an operating trust, the other three trusts use a mix of tools and both grantmaking and directly initiated operational work. JRF tends to do more operational foundation-managed work than JRRT and JRCT (in part because it has larger income). For JRCT and JRRT, directly managed work is most likely to be undertaken when there is no suitable grantee, when a wider picture is called for or when there is a need for an independent review or scoping.

Figure 7 Operating and grantmaking

Operating _____ Grantmaking

JRHT   JRF   JRRT   JRCT   'Generality' of UK trusts

This mix of grantmaking and directly initiated work raises interesting issues about the distinction between grantmaking and operating foundations.

Demonstrating feasibility/combining different types of knowledge

As discussed above, one element in the trusts' theories of change is that change requires combining different types of knowledge, including knowledge about feasibility in practice.

JRRT writes about 'appreciation for the interrelatedness of thought and action' and JRF of 'Combining the learning from our hands-on operational activity with the analytical disciplines of our wider research role, we are continuing to play our part in promoting JR's vision of healthy, neighbourly new communities' (JRCT *et al.*, 2004, p. 20). One example of this learning from testing new ideas on the ground is JRHT's pioneering of the UK's first continuing care retirement community. Another is JRF's tighter focus for PPD programmes to 'use the results of research outputs – and often our operational activities too – to achieve social change' (JRCT *et al.*, 2004, p. 26). Combining use of its demonstrations with its networks, JRF may go on to promote replication of approaches as in the case of, for example, CASPAR projects – city centre apartments for single people at affordable rents. JHRT provides an important test bed for feasibility of housing and continuing care initiatives, using the legitimacy it derives from direct experience.

Rich networks and collaboration

Figure 8 Emphasis on rich networks

High _____ Low

JRCT   JRHT   'Generality' of UK trusts

JRF

JRRT

All of the trusts recognise the power of rich networks in achieving change. As discussed above, the trusts act as brokers bringing others together to share ideas, generate knowledge and channels for communication, and create 'buy in'.

> JRCT points out that one advantage of themed programmes is that the trust is at the hub of certain wheels, with a picture of that field and relationships with others in and across fields not available to any one participant. This gives the trust networks and enables it to create networks between others. Similarly, JRF attaches significance to being well networked and invests time and money in this; its convening capacity is both a reflection of its rich networks and the basis for creation of yet wider and deeper networks.

The trusts also work closely with others inside and outside the foundation world.

Figure 9 Collaboration with other funders

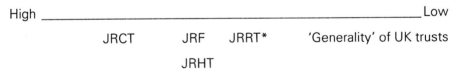

High _____ Low

| | JRCT | JRF | JRRT* | 'Generality' of UK trusts |
| | | JRHT | | |

* JRRT as a non-charitable trust has few potential collaborators.

> In recent years, there has been growing collaboration between JRRT and JRCT in which JRRT funds the campaigning and promotional activities while JRCT funds the research and educational work. Similarly, JRF and JRHT's common interest in 'poverty and place' has provided powerful collaborations.
>
> *(Continued)*

47

Outside 'the family', JRCT emphasises the value of partnerships with other UK trusts (e.g. Nuffield, Paul Hamlyn, Barrow Cadbury, Stone Ashdown) and its work with the Network of European Foundations on the European Charter of Fundamental Rights. Relationships may also be established outside the foundation world. For example, in 2003, JRF decided to build a new partnership with the Metropolitan District of Bradford in order to get closer to issues of urban renaissance and diversity. However, although JRF is without doubt very well networked, its networks are not based primarily on partnerships with other funders.

Communication

Communication is essential in moving from knowledge to social issue generation and, from there, to constructive debate and change (Ferris and Mintrom, 2002; Smith, 2002; Rogers, 2003; Bales and Gilliam, 2004). Although the trusts vary in describing themselves as having a communications strategy, they attach significance to ensuring that, where relevant, the work they fund reaches an audience. All of the trusts have invested time and resources in communication and the marketing of ideas, but have done it in different ways.

Figure 10 Approaches to communication

Direct responsibility		Devolved responsibility
JRF	JRCT	'Generality' of UK trusts
	JRRT	

While JRCT and JRRT have relied on grantees to communicate their work/issues (often with grants from the trust for that purpose), JRF has adopted a more hands-on approach, publishing and publicising work it has funded to a variety of audiences. JRF's creation of *Findings*, short-focused accounts of funded work designed to be read by busy policy makers, is now a model adopted as far afield as Australia. However, policy makers are only one potential target audience and JRF adapts its media and its message to the different needs of key players in achieving change:

Sometimes the target will be practitioners engaged indirectly in addressing social issues; often the approach will be to government Ministers, civil servants and other policy makers, with specialist seminars, face-to-face meetings, action through Parliamentary processes and background work with the news media.

(JRCT *et al.*, 2004, p. 27)

Communication is about people and networks, not just about paper.

It is worth noting here that, in 2005, the Ford Foundation announced $50 million in grants to public service media organisations in the US in order to encourage an informed citizenry and 'contribute to the public dialogue that is essential in a healthy democracy' (www.fordfound.org/news).

What works best?

In an ideal world, it would be possible to identify most effective tools and strategies for policy change. In reality, assessing the effectiveness of different approaches to achieving policy change is extraordinarily difficult, in large part because the process of policy change is complex, messy, variable and serendipitous.

As noted above, Kingdon (1984) analyses policy change in terms of problems, policies and politics. When the problem, policy and politics streams come together a subject is more likely to gain a foothold on the political agenda than if it is set in only one stream. These 'open policy windows' generally stay open only for a short time and attract a range of advocates competing for space on the government agenda (Kingdon, 1984, pp. 212–13). Kingdon also notes that, even if a problem makes it onto the political agenda, it can disappear if: the problem is attended to or cannot be solved easily; the situation changes making the problem less urgent; the problem is accepted or recast as another type of problem; other more significant problems arise; the attention cycle is exhausted (Kingdon, 1984, pp. 206–7).

In order to assess most effective ways of achieving change, it would be necessary to compare like with like. But, in the light of Kingdon's analysis, policy issues, change environments and processes vary dramatically. Thus, in order to compare like with like, it would be necessary to take into account:

- the broad characteristics of the policy environment (e.g. during some of the Thatcher years some trusts felt that there was no openness to external ideas)

- the nature of the issue (e.g. whether it is primarily technical/ operational, such as removal of VAT on wheelchairs, or ideological/divisive, such as migration policy)

- the number of policy players

- the number and strength of opponents/those with alternative change proposals

- the nature of the institutional structure/industry in which the issue is located

- the nature and strength of obstacles to change and their distribution between different groups

- the power/embeddedness of those bearing the brunt of implementing change

- the level of the issue, where power lies to achieve change and the clarity of that

- the stage of the issue in the policy process

- open or closed policy windows

- other issues on the policy agenda

- availability of opportunities for encouraging change

- the occurrence/construction of focusing events

- timing (open policy windows tend to be open only for a short time)

- the availability of feasible, affordable solutions that are not seen as presenting other, equal problems

- the foundation/grantee's existing track record on the issue/ area

- the congruence between networks/channels of communication needed and those available to the foundation/grantee

- existence of other messages/groups reinforcing demand for similar change (creating an echo chamber and strength in numbers).

Other variables could no doubt be added to this list. The point is that the efficacy of different methods and approaches is likely to vary in relation to a wide variety of factors over which the foundation has more or less influence.

Current pressures for formal performance measurement raise at least two issues for foundations engaged in policy work. First, given that achieving policy change is usually a long-term process with ups and downs and twists and turns along the way, performance measures can encourage an unhelpful, unrealistic short termism, as well as a focus on targets that may actually hamper grantees' effectiveness. The 'solution' to this problem is a high level of flexibility, trust in and interaction with grantees discussed above.

Second, performance measures raise very tricky problems of causality and attribution:

> [Some] initiatives are measurable, insofar that legislation has been introduced or agencies may be created. Much harder is the task of assessing impact in other areas such as in getting ideas into the mainstream. The positive economic benefits of migration are now openly discussed, whereas when JRCT was funding IPPR to work on these issues this was a taboo subject. The idea of Community Mediation is now widely accepted and yet it wasn't when JRCT was funding early projects in this field. Conflict transformation and peace building are now words in the wider lexicon, but they weren't a few years ago. JRCT may have played just a small part in helping organisations to bring about changes in the environment such as these.

Are the people of West Yorkshire better able to engage with civic change because of interventions funded through our West Yorkshire Racial Justice Programme? To what extent has the Peace Process in Northern Ireland been supported through the Trust's long-term backing for peacebuilding initiatives there, often on contentious issues? It is impossible to say, and yet some of these types of low key initiatives may well have been just as significant in making the world a fairer, more just and peaceful place as the higher profile work on legislation.

(S. Pittam, quoted in Anheier and Leat, 2006; see also Davies, 2004)

Foundations are further hampered in their attempt to measure their performance by lack of accepted interim indices and benchmarks for assessing progress in policy-oriented work. In the US, some measures are being developed and, in the UK, New Philanthropy Capital is embarking on a project to explore measures (further indication of the growing interest in a policy-oriented approach).

But it is also worth noting here that Ron Daniel, former managing partner of McKinsey and Company, argues that measures of performance 'have the appeal of providing measurement, but they often don't convey the essence of the phenomenon which you are trying to judge' (quoted in Cunningham and Ricks, 2004, p. 51).

Challenges and issues for policy-oriented foundations

This section discusses some of the challenges and issues faced by foundations engaged in policy-oriented work. In order to broaden the focus beyond the Rowntree trusts, it draws on interview data and published material from the Nuffield Foundation.

The uncertainty of both successful outcomes and the foundation's role in those, combined with the long-term nature of most policy work, also raises important issues about risk and exit, discussed below.

Conviction and modesty

Foundations involved in policy work have to believe that they can make a difference. This is usually a criterion for getting involved in an issue in the first place but continuing to believe is necessary to keep the foundation involved for the, usually, long haul. Because policy success is not easily attributed to any one actor, foundations engaged in policy work have to balance a conviction that they can make a difference with modesty about the difference they can make. Making a difference is different from making the difference.

> The role of Nuffield is to be a midwife. It's a snare and delusion to think that we have a great idea and can make it happen by ourselves. You've got to be modest about what you bring to the table – we're not geniuses.
>   (Interview with the Nuffield Foundation)

Risk

For reasons discussed above, foundations involved in policy-oriented work have to be willing to take risks. The challenge is to take risks without damaging reputation and relationships. But foundations in general differ in their definitions of what counts as risky and in their tolerance for risk.

Unlike the other Rowntree trusts, JRRT does not face the most commonly cited risk in relation to policy involvement – overstepping the boundaries of charity law. JRRT sees high risk as a matter of reputation and of maximising its non-charitable freedom: 'being too tame', 'doing something no one is willing to talk about', 'risking money on something that isn't timely'. But at the same time: 'We fund things because they ought to be raised – ID cards for example – not necessarily because we can win'.

JRF, JRCT and JRHT, by contrast, are constrained by charity law. In addition to that consideration, 'driven by a need to fill a knowledge gap not by desire to take on a government', JRF sees risk in terms of 'funding something there isn't time to do well in terms of the policy cycle':

> We take punts and see if we can get this on the policy agenda. The protection against risk is that the work is done well. The greatest risk for JRF is if the work is sub-standard or if it's a mode of engagement that departs from the knowledge base.

However, if change is the aim, then maintaining a consistent position on an unassailable knowledge base can be difficult.

JRCT is certainly not risk averse, and in some cases may have stepped close to the boundaries of charity law. We place ourselves deliberately at the cutting edge of difficult and contentious issues (www.jrct.org.uk). But it could be argued that it is partially protected from the consequences of the risks it takes because it more often works through its grantees than clearly and publicly branding its projects.

It is worth noting here that, while foundations that do not engage in policy-oriented work tend to cite charity law as a reason for not doing so, policy-oriented foundations do not appear to regard this as a major impediment.

Exit

There is not space to do justice to the complexity of this subject here. Because policy-oriented foundations tend to work on issues over a decade or more, difficult issues arise in striking a balance between persistence and knowing when to stop/exit either from a particular grant or from a programme/issue. When do passion and persistence become pig-headedness? When, and on what basis, is it time to admit that the timing is wrong or the strategy is going nowhere?

There is also an issue about the stage in the policy process at which a foundation should exit. Should foundations be content to work primarily at the problem-definition and agenda-setting stages or should they move into the policy-adoption phase? And, once policy has been adopted, should the foundation continue to monitor implementation?

JRF exits at various stages in the policy cycle depending on whether there is a role for it to play. Similarly, JRRT makes exit decisions on the basis of availability of opportunities 'to fund useful work'. JRCT funds work at different stages and thus exits at different stages. In some cases, JRCT may stop funding once an issue enters the mainstream debate.

The Nuffield Foundation highlights a challenge for all policy-oriented foundations wanting to ensure that policies are adopted:

To go from problem-definition and agenda-setting phases into the policy-adoption phase you need to be very, very sure and you need a lot of knowledge.

Performance measurement

Performance measurement is related to issues of exit. Without keeping track of how it is doing, how can foundations know when to reorient strategies, and ultimately when to exit? However, performance measurement has to be balanced with accepting the highs and lows of much policy work. Policy change is rarely a smooth upward trajectory (on policy change, learning and performance measurement, see Pauly, 2005).

Performance measurement also has to be balanced with the danger of over-emphasis on the measurable, and with faith and passion:

> Foundations have moved to an over-emphasis on measurement and evaluation, which has limited our passion. We put so much stress on whether you can measure it and prove it is successful that we have forgotten why we try to do the things we want to do.
>
> (Carson, 2005, p. 5)

Krehely *et al.* (2004) attribute a large part of conservative foundations' success to their willingness to take a passionately ideological stance, combined with high levels of risk taking and trust in grantees.

> It takes a leap of faith for funders to enter into the public policy arena and truly commit themselves and their resources to achieve results that may not occur for decades. But it is this type of risk-taking, hands-off approach that has made the conservative foundation involvement in public policy so effective and far-reaching.
>
> (Krehely *et al.*, 2004, p. 15)

Focus and space for creative connections

As emphasised above, for a variety of reasons, engaging with policy requires focus on a small number of issues/areas. This focus is reflected in organisational structures. The challenge is to find ways of both maintaining focus and providing 'space' for creative thinking and work. Creativity has various elements including making connections across programme boundaries and allowing for ideas from left field outside focused programme areas. Allowing space for making creative connections across programme areas is in part a matter of organisational structure and roles. Allowing space for creativity from outside the foundation is in part a matter of flexibility in grantmaking.

> Tempering focus with flexibility becomes even more important if you assume, as does the Nuffield Foundation, that there is a fluid relationship between policy and practice and that policy relevance is not always immediately apparent:
>
> > Policy issues and implications may emerge slowly or they may be there at the start. In some cases policy work may emerge out of 'good works' – it's important to keep the door open.
> >
> > We would probably say that everything we fund now has policy and practice implications – but we still want some blue skies thinking.

For this reason, it may be dangerous to become overly focused on policy relevance as a criterion in grantmaking and policy orientation as a singular style or goal.

Looking out and in

Policy-oriented foundations attach significance to constant scanning of the environment – who is doing what, how and with what effect; what is on and coming onto the policy agenda; where are the windows of opportunity to make a difference; what is Government's position; how is public opinion shifting on issues; what are the emerging issues? These are constantly changing. But, at the same time, the foundation has to balance looking out with getting on with the work.

Balancing the benefits and costs of convening

As discussed above, convening is one of the key tools used by policy-oriented foundations in the US, the UK and wider Europe that is rarely discussed in the research and practice literature (with the exception of de Borms, 2005). The different facets, roles and timing of convening require further study – as do the costs and tensions in convening.

The Nuffield Foundation notes that convening sometimes plays a role upstream before making a grant. At this stage the Nuffield convenes with applicants and others to clarify whether a project has policy and practice implications, whether the grantees have thought about it (often they have not), and to look at possibilities and what the Nuffield might do/fund.

Downstream after the grant has been made (or, in some cases, earlier), a form of convening takes place at the very start in thinking about the composition of a steering group:

We suggest getting other views and policy makers on board at the start to build support and ownership and to

(Continued)

> lay the groundwork for dissemination and communication. Voluntary organisations with policy aspirations often want to do it the other way around, packing the group with their supporters and, only after a report has been produced, going to policy makers.
>
> (Interview with the Nuffield Foundation)
>
> Later still, convening plays a role in looking at what can be done to get policy decisions made, and then putting that into effect by convening seminars, and putting people in projects in touch with policy and practice people.
>
> At every stage, convening utilises the Nuffield's networks, knowledge, credibility and reputation to bring people to the table.

Convening also involves balancing acts. What is the line between convening as providing a platform – a venue – for others and advocating a particular view? When does, or should, convening be a neutral exercise? One answer is to say that the foundation does not have a position, it funds others to have positions.

In most of what little is written about convening it is presented as a foundation playing 'honest broker'. But some foundations studied in the US were beginning to question the honesty of being an 'honest broker' once the foundation had the research and knew that, for example, a particular policy was not working (Anheier and Leat, 2006). How can the foundation balance maintaining its reputation as bipartisan, neutral 'honest broker' with being explicit about its own views and the implications of its work?

Taking a position risks greater exposure to criticism and conflict, and may reduce convening capacity in situations of conflict. On the other hand, taking a position can be powerful in using the foundation's moral and reputational legitimacy to get to change.

While JRF is considering taking a clearer position on some issues, 'being independent but not neutral', JRCT's approach is more ambivalent:

Sometimes no position is a cop-out but sometimes it enables you to get movement on contentious issues. If the aim is, say, to get to peace in Northern Ireland then taking a position on one side or the other may reduce your longer term opportunities to promote dialogue.

Similarly, JRRT talks about, in some cases, 'taking care not to frighten the horses'.

Convening also entails balancing costs and benefits. It tends to be expensive in time and human resources, and often in direct financial terms. Is convening, with all the servicing costs entailed, the best way of achieving certain objectives?

Responsibility for communication

Effective communication is essential to all policy-oriented foundations – but, again, raises difficult questions of balance. To what extent can communication be left to grantee organisations? For example, 'Academics don't always see policy and practice implications and the RAE [Research Assessment Exercise] doesn't encourage that' (interview with the Nuffield Foundation). What are the implications of leaving communications to grantees for the foundation's own reputation? This raises issues not only about quality control but also about ownership and building the foundation's public track record.

Not taking responsibility for communication is cheaper in terms of staffing and other overhead costs but it also increases the risk that effective communication does not happen. Conversely, taking direct responsibility for communication raises costs but ensures that communication happens and, in addition, adds to the foundation's reputation and brand. But it could be argued that empowering others to communicate their messages is more important than controlling the message by doing it yourself.

There are other issues. Is it desirable to have a generalised communications strategy and format to ensure consistency or do communication and dissemination have to be planned on a case-by-case basis to avoid the danger of costly and formulaic approaches?

If communication is seen as central to everything the foundation does, where does it fit in the organisational structure? And, as one foundation president in the US asked:

> Is there a danger we turn into a publishing house fed by all other departments? Does that matter? Or is it the wrong way around?

Does it matter that the foundation is widely known or that it is known only for the work it does in the right circles?

How can communication and dissemination be most effectively planned?

> Timing is very important – too early and you don't know the outcome, too late and people have moved on.
> (Interview with the Nuffield Foundation)

Issues of branding and control underlie many of these issues.

Branding

In order to establish and maintain a reputation as a credible player with specialist expertise worth listening to, to what extent do foundations need to brand their work? Establishing profile or brand is not just about outcomes of the foundation's work but also about inputs and effective use of resources.

> The Nuffield Foundation sees the use of referees as part of building its networks and brand, and influencing its inputs/applications:
>
> > Using referees is partly about informing people about what we do and the issues we are interested in. Refereeing is networking. Making a splash about funding high-profile people attracts the attention of others, builds our reputation and our networks. We've funded some key pieces of work by the best people who came to us because they knew about us. If you want to fund the best in a particular domain – such as science education – then you have to be first on everyone's list.

Having a high profile/brand not only affect inputs and the influence of outputs, but also prevent duplication of work by others. This clearly raises tricky issues about the right balance between healthy diversity/competition and wasteful, and possibly counterproductive, overlap.

> It is probably fair to say that JRF (and JRHT in housing) has the strongest brand of the four trusts. JRRT also has a strong brand but in the niche market of democratic reform. JRCT has 'huge admiration' for JRF branding but does not see building its own brand as appropriate to its more 'hands-off' style of work. (However, it might be argued that JRCT, in some measure, enjoys some of the reflected glory of the JRF brand.)
>
> However, as the Nuffield Foundation suggests, in building and maintaining its profile a foundation has to balance the extent
>
> *(Continued)*

> to which it promotes the foundation versus the issues. The dilemma is that, as JRF notes:
>
> > We're more interested in things happening than in who makes them happen but we also recognise that in order for more things to happen you need to think about reputation and brand.

Having a strong brand is likely to increase the foundation's reputational resources and power to influence change. However, a strong brand not only raises issues about ownership and control but also means that the foundation has to manage and protect its brand. One advantage of not having a strong brand is that you have no brand to lose, potentially encouraging greater risk taking and creativity.

Balancing control and enabling, operating and grantmaking

The majority of policy-oriented foundations studied to date operate some programmes/activities in house. This may be a substantive programme or it may be a function such as communications or convening. There is some anecdotal evidence that more foundations in the UK (and elsewhere) are considering bringing more of their work in house.

There are advantages to grantmaking including flexibility, lower staffing costs, borrowing expertise and so on (Leat, 2005a, 2005b). However, grantmaking also has costs and risks including loss of control over ownership and branding, as well as transaction costs. On the other hand, an operating/part-operating style entails higher staffing and other overhead costs and loss of flexibility, but greater control and more opportunities to create a strong brand. More work is needed on the costs and benefits of operating and grantmaking, why foundations choose one or the other, and how to balance the two styles.

> The Nuffield Foundation, for example, has over the years run some programmes in house:
>
> It was done for different reasons in each case. In the most recent case we are doing it in house because we have someone very good, we have clear ideas about the direction the programme should take and, in this case – but it's not often true – we think we can do it better because we have the expertise and a very interested and authoritative trustee.

Adopting a part-operating role may also enable foundations to build and utilise organisational memory, and to see crossovers and links within and across programmes that no one grantee could see. Are foundations willing and able to spend time and money on this synthesising role? What implications would this have for staffing, skills, organisational structure, knowledge acquisition and management, and relationships with grantees? This synthesising role is one to which foundations in general have tended to give little consideration, although it could be argued that it is one of their potentially most important roles (see below for further discussion).

In the light of these issues, the Nuffield Foundation describes itself as being a hybrid between an operating think tank and a grantmaking foundation, retaining the flexibility and ideas generated by grantmaking. The same description might be applied to JRF.

However, adopting an operating role is costly, even if, as discussed above, demonstrating feasibility of new approaches may also be very effective. Operating is not only costly, it also increases what some would regard as overhead costs. In addition, operating brings additional management burdens and dilemmas, as well as, particularly in service provision, reducing the flexibility of the foundation.

JRHT points out:

... the work brings with it the ongoing management responsibilities for completed projects: so the costs of embarking upon the route of 'changing by demonstrating what works' must be measured in terms of the weight of duties of care towards the people helped, for many years to come.

(It is worth noting here that the same might be said of demonstrating what works via grant-aided projects – the difference being that, when a project is grant aided, the foundation does not have direct responsibility for continuation.)

Operating programmes also raise issues about accountability, not least the question of who will act as critic of a foundation's own programme?

Collaboration

There is a view that, by working together, foundations may be more effective in achieving policy change. This is an interesting point, but probably difficult to generalise about. It raises questions of what is meant by 'collaboration'. Talk about collaboration can easily slip into statements of warm intentions and/or technical issues about the advantages and disadvantages of mergers versus joint ventures, etc. The more fundamental discussion concerns what might be gained and lost by different types of collaboration (see Table 1).

Table 1 Potential advantages and disadvantages of different types of collaboration

Type of collaboration	Potential advantages	Potential disadvantages
Sharing information about what is/might be funded at the planning stage	Avoids inefficient duplication (but not all duplication is inefficient)	Breaches confidentiality. May lead to loss of diversity
Purposely funding projects on the same or related issues (this happens already but often without knowledge and co-ordination)	Enables different aspects of the same problem or issue to be addressed. Creates echo chamber of messages	Potential for: inefficiency/duplication; mixed messages
Jointly funding the same project (this happens already but often without knowledge and co-ordination)	Shares risk. Creates larger pool of resources. Reduces risk of grantees spending time on further fundraising. May bring in new, alternative perspectives and resources	Requires clear agreements and accountability with grantees and between funders. Reduces possibility of assigning 'credit' for success. Raises issues of ownership and branding
Purposely funding different aspects or phases of the same project or issue, e.g. moving from research, to demonstration, to campaigning/advocacy (this happens already but often without knowledge and co-ordination)	Enables each funder to play to its strengths. Brings in wider and different networks. Ensures issues are followed through to achieve a sustainable outcome	Danger of different agendas of different funders/grantees. If collaboration with non-charitable funders, may raise tricky issues of charity law relating to the intentions of charitable funders. Reduces possibility of assigning 'credit' for success. Raises issues of ownership and branding

(Continued)

69

Table 1 Potential advantages and disadvantages of different types of collaboration *(Continued)*

Type of collaboration	Potential advantages	Potential disadvantages
Sharing and synthesising findings in related areas	Adds to quality and credibility of knowledge. Possible creative connections and new questions	–
Sharing communication and convening tasks	Shares workload and costs. Brings in alternative perspectives. Increases access to diverse networks. News in numbers	May reduce echo chamber effect of separate messages. Danger of different agendas of partners. Danger of mixed messages. Raises issues of ownership and leadership
Sharing thinking and practices on policy change	Efficient use of resources. Stimulates comparison, reflection and debate. Opportunities for creative thinking and crossovers. Encourages learning. Provides a focus/ information point for others interested in policy-oriented work	Raises issues of ownership. Danger of different agendas of different funders and contributors/users. Danger of being seen as an elite club

On types of collaboration, see also Knight (2005).

More work needs to be done on different types of collaboration; how and why they occur; the costs and benefits for the partners, grantees and end-users, and for the effectiveness of the project in achieving change.

Relating to Government

Relating to Government is a major challenge for policy-oriented foundations. Foundations, the public sector and political parties share a common aim: the pursuit of public benefit. Endowed foundations are potentially the least constrained of all public policy players, accountable to neither constituents, nor to donors, shareholders, customers and members. But, while endowed foundations are uniquely free to put forward alternative viewpoints, values and solutions, to risk the unpopular and unconventional, and to experiment without any terminal consequences, if they fail, they are constrained by their lack of resources and power to effect change, and by charity law. Foundations can, if they choose, challenge the priorities and programmes of Government, but they cannot alone effect the necessary changes to embed alternatives in legal and institutional policies and practices. As a result, foundations wishing to achieve sustainable change have to balance challenging Government with persuasion and enlisting support.

Opportunities and obstacles arise, not least because different parts of Government, the public sector and different political parties, as well as other public policy players such as non-profit organisations, may have different definitions of public benefit and different priorities within a broadly common definition of public benefit.

Some means of combining challenge with persuasion and support have been discussed above. For example, brokering and convening can be a means of bringing (parts of) Government to the table, increasing understanding, exposing alternative viewpoints and issues, as well as establishing some measure of ownership of the problem and its solution, building consensus and providing channels of communication.

In some cases, foundations can challenge and enlist support by acting as knowledge generators, issue entrepreneurs and risk absorbers – experimenting in areas where Government might initially fear to tread or may lack feasible solutions. In these respects civil servants and advisers may welcome foundation contributions. Foundations can also work to build constituencies for change on issues where government interventions might be counter-productive or politically risky.

For JRF, balancing challenge and support is partly about style: 'being amicable not aggressive; ensuring that the media fairly reflect the content of research; being a constructive critic'. JRF is also careful to work with both Government and Opposition, not least because, while the former is currently in a position to effect change, the latter may be in that position in the future.

JRCT works mainly at arms length from Government, funding organisations that might be working with Government (e.g. on developing the Commission for Equalities and Human Rights) and in challenging Government (e.g. on issues of asylum policy and civil liberties).

JRRT's position, as discussed above, is somewhat different, partly because it is non-charitable but also because it seeks to promote not only specific policy outcomes, but rather the democratic process itself. For JRRT, what distinguishes a democracy are the facilities for opposition and thus, in important ways, it is always working to challenge the governing party.

A recent study of foundations in Europe found that civil servants in the UK appeared to have relatively little understanding of foundations in general; and foundations themselves were aware that they have a low profile in relation to Government (Leat, forthcoming). If foundations wish to be more effective in policy work, it may be time for them to pay more attention to what they can bring to the policy table, to communicate that more effectively and to identify potential alliances and networks within the policy arena. If foundations fail to set an agenda for relations with Government, it is possible that they will find themselves increasingly responding to Government's agenda.

6 Conclusion

The potential and the characteristics of foundations engaged in creative policy work may be summarised as follows.
    'The signature characteristics of foundations:

- Resource independence

- Political independence

- Self-governance

Enable them to adopt strategies:

- Long-term investment in knowledge creation, credibility/ reputation, demonstration, learning and diffusion

- Taking up risky or neglected issues or solutions, and redefining if necessary

- Retaining flexibility and commitment in the face of cultural pressures for short-term performance measurement

- Working at multiple levels and from different angles

(Continued)

- Building rich networks across boundaries

- Building new institutions, structures and practices if necessary

And roles:

- Knowledge entrepreneurs/generators and organisers of new thinking

- Social issue entrepreneurs

- Risk absorbers

- Brokers and convenors

Which address/adopt the key characteristics of the creativity–innovation–diffusion process:

- Thinking beyond/outside the mainstream

- Controversy and new combinations

- Knowledge intensity

- Flexibility for adaptation, experimentation and learning

- Investment in diffusion

- Rich networks – homophilous and heterophilous – spanning established boundaries for creativity, implementation and diffusion'

(Anheier and Leat, 2006).

Policy-oriented foundations invest in building knowledge, reputation/authority, networks and communication. They know that ideas and values matter; that ideas can be propagated, marketed and sold; and that politics is 'a relentless intellectual contest, to be waged as an aggressive war of ideas'. They recognise that policy discourse is no longer the sole preserve of political parties, interest groups and elite opinion makers, but is now shared with the media, direct mail, talk radio, the Web, and so on. But:

> These new realities of the policy process have posed continuing, bewildering challenges to mainstream foundations whose work has been grounded in problem-oriented, field specific and, above all, pragmatic work.
> (Smith, 2002, p. 25)

These characteristics produce a very different culture, approach to resources, roles, key activities and so on from those conventionally adopted in foundations.

Differences between policy-oriented and conventional approaches

Creative, policy-oriented foundations are different from other foundations in a variety of ways. Table 2 summarises some of these differences.

Table 2 A summary of some of the differences between policy-oriented and conventional approaches

Conventional approach	Creative policy-oriented approach
Goals: doing good; helping those unable to help themselves	Sustainable change with impact beyond immediate grantees
Values and aspirations: charity; doing good	Enhancing democratic debate and the problem-solving capacity of society
Roles: filling gaps; doing good; backstop to the State; experimentation	Stimulating creative conversation and change, acting as: knowledge entrepreneurs/generators; social issue entrepreneurs; risk absorbers; brokers and convenors
Theory of change (if articulated at all): bottom-up experimentation leads to change	Explicit and often contested. Social change a mix of top-down and bottom-up; not logical, predictable or linear; a matter of iteration not cataclysm; requires work at various levels and multiple strategies. No 'one size fits all' theory – depends on the issue
Approach to resources: money seen as major resource; and, for some, management skills	Money seen as means to capitalise on knowledge, networks and influence as key resources
Approach to planning and management: seen as means of strategic control	Leadership not management. Plan as a flexible point of departure. Opportunism as part of strategy
Key activities: making grants	Grantmaking a means to an end of generating new solutions to problems via knowledge, demonstration, networks and communication. Making connections between people, power and ideas. Variety of activities to reach groups who have a bearing on the outcome

(Continued)

77

Table 2 A summary of some of the differences between policy-oriented and conventional approaches (Continued)

Conventional approach	Creative policy-oriented approach
Funding policies and practices: short-term grants; let 1,000 flowers bloom; silo funding	Long-term or as long as it takes; smaller number of issues and grantees; funding across boundaries
Relationship with grantees: distanced, short-term, 'feudal', paternalist, neutral/low-trust	Closer, longer-term, 'partnership', higher-trust
Approach to risk: ambiguous – lip service but generally something to be avoided	Essential part of creativity and innovation
Approach to performance measurement: focused on short-term success and failure	Longer-term, flexible, opportunity for learning
Relationship with Government: generally to be avoided	Important part of a range of relationships
Approach to policy making: something politicians do and 'not for us'	Policy making the outcome of a complex 'war' of ideas in a competitive, crowded marketplace to which foundations may contribute
Relationship to wider environment and others: inward-looking, independent, insulated	Outward-looking, adaptive, flexible, working with others a key activity

Adapted from Anheier and Leat, 2006.

REFERENCES

Anheier, H.K. and Daly, S. (forthcoming) *Foundations in Europe: Roles and Visions.* London: Routledge

Anheier, H.K. and Leat, D. (2002) *From Charity to Creativity: Philanthropic Foundations for the 21st Century.* Stroud: Comedia.

Anheier, H.K. and Leat, D. (2006) *Creative Philanthropy.* London: Routledge

Aron, N. (2002) 'Funding nonprofit advocacy: the increasing role of foundations', in R. Cohen (ed.) *The State of Philanthropy.* Washington, DC: NCRP

Bailin, M. (2003) 'Re-engineering philanthropy: field notes from the trenches', in *Waldemar A. Nielsen Issues in Philanthropy Seminar Series.* Center for the Study of Voluntary Organizations and Service at Georgetown University. Washington, DC

Bales, S.N. and Gilliam, F.D. (2004) *Practice Matters Improving Philanthropy Project.* www.fdncenter.org/for_grantmakers/practice_matters/

de Borms, L.T. (2005) *Foundations Creating Impact in a Globalised World.* London: John Wiley and Sons

Brousseau, R.T. (2004) *Experienced Grantmakers at Work: When Creativity Comes into Play.* New York, NY: The Foundation Center

Burkeman, S. (2004) 'Influencing public policy', in Millfield House Foundation *Funding Policy Change for a Better Society in the North East of England.* Newcastle upon Tyne: Millfield House Foundation

Burkeman, S. and Harker, A. (2005) 'Stepping up the stairs', unpublished paper

Carson, E. (2005) 'The cost of caution: advocacy, public policy and America's foundations', speech in Georgetown University Center for Public and Nonprofit Leadership, 21 April, http://cpnl.georgetown.edu

Coleman, J.S., Menzel, H. and Katz, E. (1957) 'The diffusion of an innovation among physicians', *Sociometry*, Vol. 20, pp. 253–70

Cunningham, K. and Ricks, M. (2004) 'Why measure?', *Stanford Social Innovation Review*, summer, p. 51

Davies, J. (2004) 'The foundation as a policy actor: the case of the Joseph Rowntree Charitable Trust', *The Political Quarterly*, Vol. 75, Issue 3, pp. 275–84

Ferris, J.M. and Mintrom, M. (2002) 'Foundations and public policy making: a conceptual framework', RP-10, May, www.usc.edu/philanthropy

Gordon, I., Lewis, J. and Young, K. (1997) 'Perspectives on policy analysis', in M. Hill (ed.) *The Policy Process, A Reader.* London: Prentice Hall/Harvester Wheatsheaf

Heifetz, R.A, Kania J.V. and Kramer, M.R. (2004) 'Leading boldly', *Stanford Social Innovation Review*, winter, pp. 21–32

JRCT, JRF and JRRT (2004) *The Joseph Rowntree Inheritance 1904–2004.* York: JRCT, JRF, JRRT

JRRT (2004) *Trusting in Change: A Story of Reform.* York: JRRT

Kanter, R.M. (1983) *The Change Masters.* New York, NY: Simon and Schuster

Kanter, R.M., Stein, B.A. and Jick, T.D. (1992) *The Challenge of Organisational Change.* New York, NY: Free Press

Kendall, J. and Anheier, H. (1999) 'The third sector and the European Union policy process: an initial evaluation', *Journal of European Public Policy Process*, Vol. 6, No. 2, pp. 283–307

Kingdon, J.W. (1984) *Agendas, Alternatives and Public Policies.* New York, NY: HarperCollins

Knight, B. (2005) *Social Justice, Poverty Reduction and Inclusive Communities, The Role of Independent Charitable Trusts and Foundations.* A report to the Barrow Cadbury Trust. Newcastle upon Tyne: CENTRIS

Kramer, M. (2005) 'Scaling social impact', *Foundation Strategy Group Perspectives for Private Foundations*, winter

Krehely, J., House, M. and Kernan, E. (2004) *Axis of Ideology: Conservative Foundations and Public Policy.* Washington, DC: NCRP

Landry, C. (2000) *The Creative City: A Toolkit for Urban Innovators.* London: Comedia, Earthscan Publications Ltd

Leat, D. (2005a) *A Discussion Paper on Risk and Good Grantmaking.* Big Lottery Fund Research Issue 17. London: Big Lottery Fund

Leat, D. (2005b) 'Theories of social change: background paper', in D. Eilinghoff (ed.) *Rethinking Philanthropic Effectiveness.* Gtersloh: Verlag Betelsmann Stiftung

Leat, D. (forthcoming) 'Britain', in H.K. Anheier and S. Daly (eds) *Foundations in Europe: Roles and Visions.* London: Routledge

NCRP (National Committee for Responsive Philanthropy) (1997) *Moving a Public Policy Agenda: The Strategic Philanthropy of Conservative Foundations.* Washington, DC: NCRP. www.ncrp.org

NCRP (National Committee for Responsive Philanthropy) (2003) *Understanding Social Justice Philanthropy*. Washington, DC: NCRP

Palmer, G., North, J., Carr, J. and Kenway, P. (2003) *Monitoring Poverty and Social Exclusion*. York: Joseph Rowntree Foundation

Pauly, E. (2005) 'The role of evaluation in the 21st century foundation', in D. Eilinghoff (ed.) *Rethinking Philanthropic Effectiveness*. Gtersloh: Verlag Betelsmann Stiftung

Pfeffer, J. (2001) 'To build a culture of innovation, avoid conventional management wisdom', in F. Hessselbein, M. Goldsmith and I. Somerville (eds) *Leading for Innovation and Organizing for Results*. New York, NY: Jossey Bass

Prewitt, K. (1999) 'The importance of foundations in an open society', in A. Schluter, V. Then and P. Walkenhorst (eds) *Foundations in Europe Society Management and Law*. London: Directory of Social Change

Roelofs, J. (2003) *Foundations and Public Policy: The Mask of Pluralism*. New York, NY: State University of New York Press

Rogers, E.M. (2003) *Diffusion of Innovations*. New York, NY: Free Press

Rosenman, M. (1998) 'A return to alms: commentary on the report of the National Commission on Philanthropy and Civic Renewal', in D.S. Gardner (ed.) *Vision and Values: Rethinking the Nonprofit Sector in America*. A report for the Nathan Cummings Foundation. New York, NY: Nathan Cummings Foundation in association with PONPO

Rosenman, M. (2005) 'Grantmakers must focus on Government's role', *The Chronicle of Philanthropy*, 17 February

Smith, J.A. (2002) *Foundations and Public Policy Making: A Historical Perspective*. www.usc.edu/philanthropy

Tomei, A. (1998) 'Foundations active or reactive?', unpublished paper delivered at The Hague Club Meeting, September

Appendix: Achievements of policy-oriented foundations

Although it is difficult to attribute change to any one factor, foundations engaged with policy have made important contributions in achieving sustainable change with impacts beyond their immediate grantees.

In the US the tradition of policy engagement goes back to at least 1867 when George Peabody endowed the Peabody Education Fund to work to create public education in the South. Indeed, all of the large foundations established in the early twentieth century in the US (Russell Sage, Carnegie, Rockefeller, Rosenwald and Commonwealth) not only shared a vision of making philanthropy more efficient but also understood that they had to engage Government (Smith, 2002). Although somewhat muted in recent years, that tradition of engaging with Government continues.

The California Wellness Foundation

In 1992, the California Wellness Foundation began funding groups advocating reduction of youth access to guns and for increased support for youth violence prevention programmes. Over the last decade, the number of firearm deaths in California has almost halved and there has been a huge increase in government funding for youth violence prevention:

(Continued)

That funding increase plainly owes much to the vigorous advocacy of Wellness Foundation supported charities. (Center for Lobbying in the Public Interest [clpi], www.clpi.org)

The Rosenberg Foundation

The Rosenberg Foundation played a major part in achieving reform of the child welfare support system in California. In addition, it has contributed to strengthening the low-wage sector of the labour market by enforcing labour laws and reducing the likelihood that immigrant workers will erode wages and conditions for all workers, by persuading the Social Security Administration to modify its practices regarding discrepancies in Social Security numbers to reduce unnecessary termination of immigrant workers; obtaining substantial awards of unpaid back wages and overtime for low-wage and immigrant workers in several industries and expanding the concept of joint-employer liability for substandard practices; increasing the use of wage and job quality criteria for the allocation of public subsidies for economic development; and increased access to public services for language minorities in California (Anheier and Leat, 2005).

Many other US foundations could be added including: the Ford Foundation in various fields; the Wallace Foundation in the field of education; Annie E. Casey Foundation in childcare; the Pew Charitable Trusts in, among other areas, the environment; and the Knight Foundation in journalism. In the UK, the examples are fewer but include: the Nuffield Foundation; Esmee Fairbairn Foundation; Carnegie UK Trust; Diana, Princess of Wales Memorial Fund; and others.

Nuffield Foundation

The Nuffield Foundation is a charitable organisation. The majority of its income is spent on research, practical innovation and policy development in social policy, education and science. Education is its major theme and it spends one-third of its funds on schemes that support young researchers. The Nuffield's interest in policy relevance is clearly stated in its preferences:

> The Foundation looks to support projects that are imaginative and innovative, take a thoughtful and rigorous approach to problems, and have the potential to influence policy or practice.
>
> (www.nuffieldfoundation.org)

The Nuffield runs a number of grant programmes for specific purposes, currently focusing on:

1 child protection, family law and justice – helping to ensure that the legal and institutional framework best meets the needs of children and families

2 access to justice – promoting access to, and understanding of, the civil justice system

3 older people and their families – promoting the autonomy and well-being of older people by developing policy and practice.

In addition, the Nuffield maintains an 'open-door' programme to allow for funding of cross-programme or innovative projects.

In some cases, the Nuffield operates projects of its own. The two largest relate to bioethics and the curriculum.

(Continued)

One of the Nuffield's achievements was in the 1980s when it supported the development of integrated schools in Northern Ireland (with JRCT), later adopted by Government. Among its more recent areas of influence have been developments in science education and the curriculum, as well the outputs of the Nuffield Council on Bioethics, which has largely set the agenda for debate on such issues.

The Diana, Princess of Wales Memorial Fund

The Fund was an important player in the period leading up to the Convention of Conventional Weapons Annual Meeting of States Parties in the Hague at which a legally binding protocol relating to the clearing up of unexploded cluster bomblets was adopted.

In addition, the Fund, in association with the All-Party Parliamentary Group on AIDS and Help the Hospices Fund, organised a dialogue between practitioners of palliative care in Africa and other organisations working in HIV/AIDS prevention and care. The aim was to bring together two groups of professionals working to the same end but with little previous collaboration. Dr Joseph F. O'Neill, Deputy Global Aids Co-ordinator at the US Department of State, one of the speakers, has paid tribute to the work of the Fund:

> The vision and models of care that sprang from [the Fund's] effort formed a cornerstone of the US Government's President's Emergency Plan for Aids Relief – a $15 billion program that will spend over $2 billion on palliative care in Africa, The Caribbean and Asia. In my view, we are standing on the shoulders of the Diana Fund's efforts in regard to palliative care and should recognize their work as an example of the ways that private philanthropic initiatives can positively influence government policy.
>
> (Quoted in Anheier and Leat, 2006)

For examples of the achievements of other US and UK foundations engaged with policy see Anheier and Leat (2006).